EARTHQUAKES

MEREDITH OWENS

NEW YORK

Published in 2017 by The Rosen Publishing Group, Inc.
29 East 21st Street, New York, NY 10010

Editor: Melissa Raé Shofner
Book Design: Michael Flynn
Interior Layout: Mickey Harmon

Photo Credits: Cover (image) Perfect Gui/Shutterstock.com; p. 5 Yai/Shutterstock.com; p. 6 Lukiyanova Natalia/frenta/ Shutterstock.com; p. 7 Peter Hermes Furian/Shutterstock.com; p. 9 James P. Blair/Getty Images; p. 11 Naypong/ Shutterstock.com; p. 12 Inga Spence/Getty Images; p. 13 NYPL/Science Source/Getty Images; p. 15 Russell Curtis/ Getty Images; p. 17 David Hume Kennerly/Getty Images; p. 19 (city hall destroyed) courtesy of the Library of Congress; p. 19 (city hall) https://commons.wikimedia.org/wiki/File:SF_City_Hall.jpg p. 21 Jens Lambert/Shutterstock.com; p. 22 Skip ODonnell/Getty Images.

Library of Congress Cataloging-in-Publication Data

Names: Owens, Meredith P., author.
Title: Earthquakes / Meredith Owens.
Description: New York : PowerKids Press, [2017] | Series: Spotlight on Earth
  science | Includes index.
Identifiers: LCCN 2016025365| ISBN 9781499426182 (pbk.) | ISBN 9781499426168 (library bound) | ISBN 9781499425062 (6 pack)
Subjects: LCSH: Earthquakes--Juvenile literature.
Classification: LCC QE521.3 .O944 2017 | DDC 551.22--dc23
LC record available at https://lccn.loc.gov/2016025365

Manufactured in China

CPSIA Compliance Information: Batch #BW17PK For further information contact Rosen Publishing, New York, New York at 1-800-237-9932.

CONTENTS

CHAPTER ONE

SHAKY GROUND

If the ground under your feet ever starts to shake suddenly, it might be an earthquake. Earthquakes are natural events that happen all the time. In fact, there are hundreds of small earthquakes around the world each day. These small quakes don't cause **damage** and often go unnoticed. Sometimes scientists' machines don't even register them!

Bigger quakes are definitely felt. They can cause **destruction** and even death. Several big earthquakes may happen each month. You might see news of such **disasters** on television. These strong quakes can leave an area in ruins. To make matters worse, earthquakes often cause other natural disasters.

Scientists don't know when or where earthquakes will strike. However, they do know a lot about what happens before, during, and after a quake. Read on to learn more about these powerful natural disasters.

This building in Chile was damaged during an earthquake in 2010.

CHAPTER TWO

MOVING PLATES

Earth has four main layers: the crust, mantle, outer **core**, and inner core. The crust and the top part of the mantle form the lithosphere. The lithosphere is broken into large plates that fit together like puzzle pieces. The plates "float" on top of a layer of mostly melted rock.

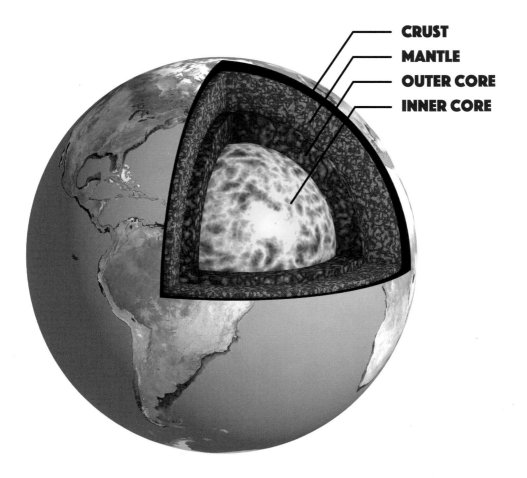

CRUST

MANTLE

OUTER CORE

INNER CORE

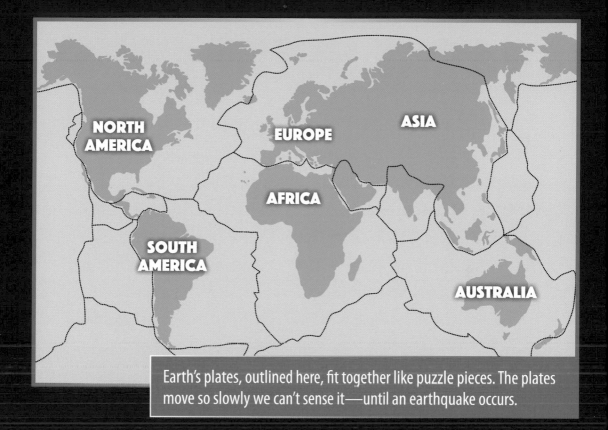

Earth's plates, outlined here, fit together like puzzle pieces. The plates move so slowly we can't sense it—until an earthquake occurs.

Earth's plates are constantly moving. Some drift apart, while others move toward or past each other. The edges of the plates are not smooth, so they often get stuck together, creating **friction**. The energy created is stored up, sometimes for hundreds of years.

When the plates suddenly slip past each other, the stored energy escapes. This causes an earthquake. Some sections of crust have become used to constant movement. They grind slowly past each other instead of becoming stuck. This causes many small shocks and **tremors** rather than one major earthquake.

CHAPTER THREE

CRACKS IN THE CRUST

Cracks form in Earth's crust as the plates move and bump each other. These cracks are called faults. Faults are found along plate boundaries, but they can also form elsewhere. They can be less than an inch (2.5 cm) to more than 1,000 miles (1,609 km) long. Many faults are below the surface and can't be seen. When a fault appears on Earth's surface, it's called a fault line.

There are three main types of faults: normal, **reverse**, and strike-slip. When a piece of crust moves downward and away from another piece, the result is called a normal fault. A reverse fault occurs when a piece of crust moves upward and toward another piece. Two pieces moving side by side in opposite directions cause a strike-slip fault.

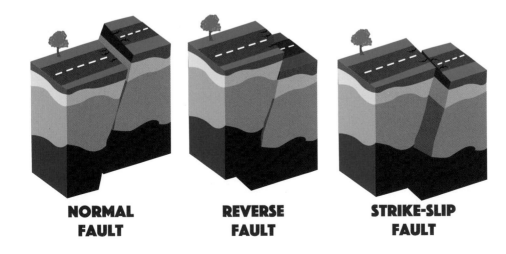

NORMAL FAULT   **REVERSE FAULT**   **STRIKE-SLIP FAULT**

The San Andreas Fault in California is a strike-slip fault. Many powerful earthquakes happen here.

Earthquakes occur along faults. The spot within Earth where an earthquake starts is called the hypocenter. The epicenter is the place on Earth's surface right above the hypocenter.

CHAPTER FOUR

ROCKY WAVES

The stored energy released, or let go, during an earthquake travels away from the epicenter in all directions. The energy vibrates, or moves back and forth quickly. These vibrations are called seismic waves.

Seismic waves deep within Earth are called body waves. There are two types of body waves: primary (or P waves) and secondary (or S waves). "Primary" means "first," and P waves are the first to be felt. They travel fast, pushing and pulling their way through solids and liquids. S waves move up and down or from side to side. They're slower and can't move through liquids.

Seismic waves in Earth's crust are called surface waves. They arrive last and cause the most damage. Surface waves also move the ground up and down and from side to side. Earthquakes that start deeper in the earth create weaker surface waves and cause less damage.

P WAVES

S WAVES

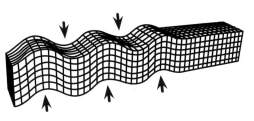

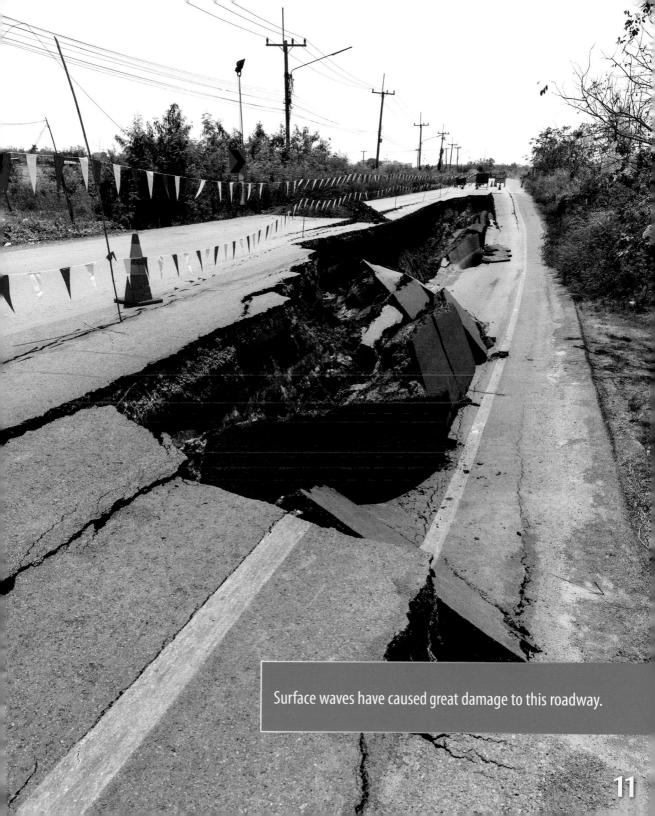

Surface waves have caused great damage to this roadway.

CHAPTER FIVE

MEASURING QUAKES

Seismologists are scientists who study earthquakes and seismic waves. They measure these waves to figure out where an earthquake started and how big it was. When the ground shakes during an earthquake, a machine called a seismograph records the seismic waves as squiggly lines.

Seismic waves are strongest at the epicenter of an earthquake. They get weaker as they move farther away. Seismologists can look at recordings from different seismograph stations to find the epicenter.

Foreshocks are tremors that happen before a larger earthquake. Scientists don't know that a quake is a foreshock until a bigger earthquake occurs. Aftershocks are tremors that happen in the days, weeks, and months following a big quake. Earthquakes that occur closer to the surface are more likely to have aftershocks.

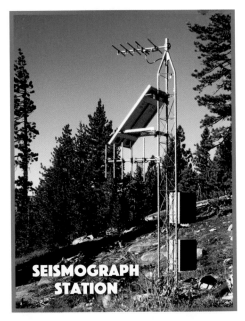

SEISMOGRAPH STATION

Charles Richter, an American seismologist, learned about movement within the earth by studying seismograph recordings. He created the Richter scale in 1935.

Seismologists also look at seismograph readings to figure out the **magnitude** of an earthquake. Magnitude used to be measured using the Richter scale, which was created by Charles Richter in 1935. Each whole number on the scale stands for a magnitude 10 times greater than the whole number before it. For example, a magnitude 5.0 earthquake is 10 times more powerful than a magnitude 4.0 earthquake.

RICHTER SCALE		
MAGNITUDE	**EFFECTS**	**EARTHQUAKES PER YEAR**
8.0–8.9	SEVERE DAMAGE AND LOSS OF LIFE OVER LARGE AREAS	FEWER THAN 3
7.0–7.9	SERIOUS DAMAGE OVER LARGE AREAS; LOSS OF LIFE	3 TO 20
6.0–6.9	INCREASED DAMAGE TO POPULATED AREAS	20 TO 200
5.0–5.9	SOME DAMAGE TO WEAK BUILDINGS	200 TO 2,000
4.0–4.9	FELT BY EVERYONE; MINOR DAMAGE	2,000 TO 12,000
3.0–3.9	FELT BY MANY PEOPLE; NO DAMAGE	12,000 TO 100,000
LESS THAN 2.9	NOT USUALLY FELT BY PEOPLE	MORE THAN 100,000

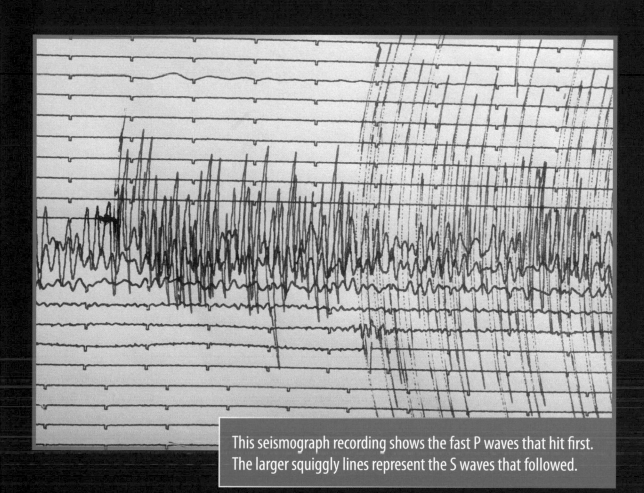

This seismograph recording shows the fast P waves that hit first. The larger squiggly lines represent the S waves that followed.

More powerful earthquakes are higher on the scale. These earthquakes release more energy and cause more damage. People rarely even notice quakes that are below a magnitude 3.0 on the Richter scale.

A newer way of measuring the strength of an earthquake is the moment magnitude scale, or MMS. Compared to the Richter scale, the MMS is more exact. It measures the total energy of an earthquake by looking at three ways the earth moved when it hit.

CHAPTER SIX

DESTRUCTIVE DISASTERS

Earthquakes can cause a lot of damage. Buildings and bridges can fall down. Roadways can shift or crumble. People can be hurt or even killed. Earthquakes often cause other natural disasters that lead to even more destruction.

Aftershocks may occur as Earth's crust settles back into place. Each aftershock is weaker than the one before it, but additional damage can still happen. Earthquakes can also cause rocks, soil, and other **debris** to slide down slopes. Structures and people can be buried or swept away in these landslides. Fires can occur if gas lines or electrical wires are damaged during a quake. Candles, stoves, and fireplaces can also start fires.

An underwater earthquake can cause a tsunami, or giant wave. Tsunamis may travel thousands of miles across the ocean. These powerful waves can drown people, flood the land, and destroy many structures.

In 1994, an earthquake in Los Angeles, California, caused fire and flooding.

CHAPTER SEVEN

EARTHQUAKE EFFECTS

Earthquakes can have lasting social, economic, and **environmental** impacts on an area. Fallen rocks or land that has been lowered can change the flow of waterways. Wild plants and animals can be killed, which can throw the local **ecosystem** off balance. Important landmarks can be damaged or destroyed.

The loss of crops and livestock can cause economic problems. Clean drinking water may also be hard to find. There can be chemical spills or damage to nuclear power plants. Many people may be left without homes or jobs. Electricity and communications systems may be knocked out. Buildings, roads, and bridges may need to be rebuilt.

Recovering from a major earthquake can be very hard. Organizations like the American Red Cross and UNICEF provide as much disaster relief as they can. People from around the world send supplies and money to help.

A postcard from the early 1900s shows San Francisco City Hall before the 1906 earthquake. The building was supposed to be earthquake-proof, but it collapsed within seconds during the quake, as seen in the photograph above.

CHAPTER EIGHT

NOT ALL NATURAL

Earthquakes are natural disasters, but sometimes humans cause them, too. Man-made quakes aren't usually very powerful. A few in the magnitude 5.0 to 6.0 range have been reported, but most are magnitude 3.0 to 4.0 earthquakes or smaller. In the United States, the average number of magnitude 3.0 or higher earthquakes has greatly increased in recent years. Human impact on the environment might be to blame.

FRACKING

Engineers pump water, sand, and chemicals through the earth at high pressure. This creates fractures, or cracks, in the rock and releases trapped natural gas.

Problems arise when people add or remove liquids or gases from the earth. New cracks in Earth's crust can be made and existing cracks can become larger. The pressure inside the crust is also affected. Processes like **fracking** and the storage of **carbon dioxide** within the earth might cause quakes. Mining leaves empty spaces within the earth. Filling man-made **reservoirs** adds extra weight to the crust. These changes can also put pressure on new or existing cracks.

CHAPTER NINE

STAYING SAFE

Knowing how to stay safe during an earthquake is very important. Most people are hurt by falling debris. Find a safe place to take cover, such as under a sturdy table or desk. Stay away from walls, windows, or tall furniture that could break or fall on you. If you're outside, move to an open area away from trees, buildings, and power lines.

It helps to be prepared before an earthquake hits. If you live in an area where quakes commonly occur, create an earthquake kit with food, drinking water, flashlights, and medical supplies. Keep the kit where it can be easily reached. It's also a good idea to know how to turn off the gas, water, and electricity in your home in case the lines break. Figure out a safe place in every room and practice dropping to the floor, taking cover, and holding on to a sturdy object.

Create an earthquake kit with supplies like these. Don't forget extra batteries.

GLOSSARY

carbon dioxide (KAR-buhn dy-AHK-syd) A colorless and odorless gas vital to life on Earth.

core (KOR) The center of something.

damage (DAA-midj) Loss or harm done to a person or piece of property.

debris (duh-BREE) Broken pieces of objects or objects left somewhere because they are not wanted.

destruction (deh-STRUK-shun) The state of being destroyed or ruined.

disaster (dih-ZAS-tuhr) Something that happens suddenly and causes much suffering and loss for many people.

ecosystem (EE-koh-sys-tuhm) All the living things in an area.

environment (in-VY-run-munt) The conditions that surround a living thing and affect the way it lives.

fracking (FRA-king) Pushing water, sand, and chemicals through the earth at high pressure to free up resources such as oil and natural gas.

friction (FRIK-shun) The force that resists motion between bodies in contact.

magnitude (MAG-nuh-tood) A measure of the power of an earthquake.

reservoir (REH-suh-vwar) A man-made lake used for storing water.

reverse (rih-VERS) Opposite to what is usual or normal.

tremor (TREH-muhr) A shaking movement before or after an earthquake.

INDEX

PRIMARY SOURCE LIST

Page 13
Charles Francis Richter. Photograph. ca. 1970s. From NYPL/Science Source, Getty Images.

Page 15
Seismograph recording of the Loma Prieta earthquake. Northern California. October 17, 1989. Recorded in Columbia, CA. Photo by Russell Curtis. From Getty Images.

Page 19
(Top) Pre-earthquake San Francisco City Hall. Postcard. Created by Goeggel and Weidner Publishers, San Francisco, CA. ca. 1900. (Bottom) Post-earthquake San Francisco City Hall. Photograph by Alex L. Murat. 1906. Now kept at the Library of Congress Prints and Photographs Division, Washington, DC.

WEBSITES

Due to the changing nature of Internet links, PowerKids Press has developed an online list of websites related to the subject of this book. This site is updated regularly. Please use this link to access the list: www.powerkidslinks.com/soes/quakes